D1036976

The Undertaker

Pro Wrestler
Mark Callaway

by A. R. Schaefer

Reading Consultant:
Dr. Robert Miller
Professor of Special Education
Minnesota State University, Mankato

CAPSTONE
HIGH-INTEREST
BOOKS

an imprint of Capstone Press
Mankato, Minnesota

Capstone High-Interest Books are published by Capstone Press
151 Good Counsel Drive, P.O. Box 669, Mankato, Minnesota 56002
http://www.capstone-press.com

Library of Congress Cataloging-in-Publication Data
Schaefer, A. R. (Adam Richard), 1976–
   The Undertaker : pro wrestler Mark Callaway/by A.R. Schaefer.
   p. cm.—(Pro wrestlers)
   Summary: Traces the personal life and career of professional wrestler
Mark Callaway, who is known as the Undertaker.
   Includes bibliographical references (p. 45) and index.
   ISBN 0-7368-1312-8 (hardcover)
   1. Undertaker, 1965– —Juvenile literature. 2. Wrestlers—United
States—Biography—Juvenile literature. [1. Undertaker, 1965– 2. Wrestlers.]
I. Title. II. Series.
GV1196.U54 S35 2003
796.812'092—dc21   2001008112

Editorial Credits
Angela Kaelberer, editor; Karen Risch, product planning editor; Timothy Halldin,
   series designer; Gene Bentdahl, book designer; Jo Miller, photo researcher

Photo Credits
Dr. Michael Lano, cover (all), 4, 7, 10, 15, 16, 18, 21, 22, 25, 26, 29, 30, 33, 34, 40
George DeSota/Getty Images, 42
Rich Freeda/Getty Images, 36, 39
Texas Wesleyan University, 13

1 2 3 4 5 6 07 06 05 04 03 02

Capstone Press thanks Dr. Michael Lano, WReaLano@aol.com, for his assistance
in the preparation of this book.

Table of Contents

Chapter 1   WWF Champion 5

Chapter 2   The Early Years 11

Chapter 3   Early Success........................... 19

Chapter 4   WWF Star 27

Chapter 5   The Undertaker Today 37

Features

Major Matches 9

The Undertaker's Hero 15

Rival in the Ring 30

Career Highlights 43

Words to Know 44

To Learn More 45

Useful Addresses 46

Internet Sites 47

Index 48

Chapter 1

WWF Champion

On November 27, 1991, professional wrestling fans filled Joe Louis Arena in Detroit, Michigan. The World Wrestling Federation (WWF) was in Detroit for Survivor Series.

That night, one of the WWF's most popular wrestlers was defending his World Championship title. That wrestler was Terry Bollea. Bollea wrestles as Hulk Hogan. Hogan's opponent was Mark Callaway. He wrestles as the Undertaker.

A Dark Character

Mark wore a long black coat and thick gray gloves. A black hat covered much of his face.

Wrestlers play different roles during their matches. Some wrestlers are heroes. They are

Mark wore thick gray gloves as part of his costume.

5

called "babyfaces" or "faces." Others act mean to the fans or to other wrestlers. These wrestlers are called "heels." At the 1991 Survivor Series, Hogan was a babyface. Mark was a heel, but many of the fans at Survivor Series cheered for him.

Early Action
Early in the match, Mark choked Hogan with a TV cable outside the ring. The referee almost disqualified Mark. Hogan would have won the match if Mark had been disqualified. But Mark let go of Hogan before the referee could rule against him.

Mark put his hands over Hogan's mouth and nose. Hogan broke free. Mark then took Hogan down with one of his signature moves. This move is called the Tombstone Piledriver. Mark picked up Hogan and held him upside down by the legs. He then slammed Hogan's neck to the mat. Hogan was not ready to give up. He got up and slammed Mark to the mat.

Help from a Friend
Mark's manager, William Moody, was outside the ring. He was known as Paul Bearer. Bearer

Mark's manager, Paul Bearer, helped Mark during his match against Hulk Hogan.

grabbed Hogan's leg. Richard Fliehr then ran up to the ring. Fliehr wrestles as Ric Flair. Flair grabbed Hogan's World Champion belt from the ring.

Hogan chased Flair around the ring. Hogan then jumped back into the ring. He kicked Mark in the face and tried to take Mark down with a legdrop. Bearer grabbed Hogan's legs. Mark grabbed Hogan by the throat and choked him.

Mark then lifted Hogan into the air for the Tombstone Piledriver. At the same time, Flair threw a metal chair into the ring. Mark slammed Hogan's body down on the chair. This time, he covered Hogan. The referee counted to three. Mark was the new WWF World Champion.

About Mark Callaway

Mark Callaway is 6 feet, 10 inches (208 centimeters) tall. He weighs 328 pounds (149 kilograms).

Mark began his wrestling career in 1985. He joined the WWF in 1990. Mark has won the WWF World Championship three times. He also has won the WWF Tag Team title six times with four different partners.

In 2001, the WWF bought World Championship Wrestling (WCW). Mark then teamed with Glen Jacobs to win the WCW Tag Team title. Jacobs wrestles as Kane. Later that year, Mark became the WWF Hardcore Champion.

Major Matches

November 27, 1991—Mark defeats Hulk Hogan to win his first WWF World Championship.

March 23, 1997—Mark defeats Sid Vicious to win the WWF World Championship for a second time.

June 28, 1998—Mark defeats Mankind in one of the WWF's most famous cage matches.

July 26, 1998—Mark teams with "Stone Cold" Steve Austin to win the WWF Tag Team title.

May 23, 1999—Mark defeats Steve Austin to win his third WWF World Championship.

April 17, 2001—Mark teams with Kane to win the WWF Tag Team Championship.

August 7, 2001—Mark and Kane win the WCW Tag Team Championship.

August 19, 2001—Mark and Kane win their second WWF Tag Team title.

December 9, 2001—Mark defeats Rob Van Dam to win the WWF Hardcore Championship.

Chapter 2

The Early Years

Mark Callaway was born March 24, 1965. He grew up in Houston, Texas. Mark's parents are Frank and Catherine Callaway. He has a brother named Anthony.

Mark was a good athlete in high school. He played both basketball and football.

College Athlete

In 1983, Mark left home to attend college. He began classes at Angelina College in Lufkin, Texas. Angelina is a two-year college. Mark went to school and played basketball for two years at Angelina. He was a good player for the Roadrunners.

Mark was born March 24, 1965.

I never talked to that coach again...
I'd actually like to see him.
I'd say he did me a favor.
—Mark Callaway, *Dallas Morning News,* 10/8/99

In 1985, Mark finished his studies at Angelina. Mark wanted to keep playing basketball and earn a four-year college degree. Texas Wesleyan University (TWU) offered Mark a basketball scholarship. This college is in Fort Worth, Texas. Mark played center for the TWU Rams during the 1985–86 season.

During college, Mark attended professional wrestling matches. He met people who were in the wrestling business. Mark started training to become a professional wrestler. He planned to play one more season of basketball at TWU. After graduation, he wanted to become a professional wrestler.

Important Decision

In 1986, Mark's coach talked to him before basketball season started. He wanted Mark to forget about wrestling until after the season. Mark believed he had a better future in wrestling than he did in basketball. He quit college to concentrate on wrestling.

Mark played center on Texas Wesleyan University's basketball team.

Mark trained as a wrestler during the day and worked at a bar at night. He did not make much money, but he was learning about professional wrestling.

Mark started working as an independent wrestler. He wrestled at small shows attended by a few hundred fans. Many times, he did not make enough money to buy his gasoline to and from the event.

Master of Pain

In 1989, Mark got a job with the United States Wrestling Alliance (USWA). This wrestling organization had companies in Memphis, Tennessee, and Dallas, Texas. The USWA was not as large or as well known as the WWF. But Mark would have the chance to wrestle in front of thousands of people. He also would make more money.

In Memphis, Mark began wrestling for the USWA as Master of Pain. Mark was bigger and stronger than almost every other wrestler in the USWA. He also was quick and had good balance in the ring. Mark often walked across the top rope as he prepared to leap on an opponent.

First Titles

On April 1, 1989, Mark faced Jerry "The King" Lawler for the USWA Unified Heavyweight Championship. The match took place in Memphis. Lawler was one of the USWA's most popular wrestlers. Mark defeated Lawler to win his first professional wrestling

The Undertaker's Hero: Fritz Von Erich

As Mark grew up in Texas, he often watched Fritz Von Erich wrestle.

Von Erich's real name was Jack Adkisson. He won several wrestling championships during his long career. These titles included three National Wrestling Alliance (NWA) U.S. Heavyweight Championships and two NWA World Heavyweight Championships.

Von Erich owned a wrestling company in Dallas, Texas. It was called World Class Championship Wrestling (WCCW). Mark wrestled some matches for WCCW in the late 1980s. Von Erich died of cancer in 1997.

Von Erich's sons also were professional wrestlers. His sons' names were David, Mike, Chris, Kevin, and Kerry. Mark wrestled Kerry Von Erich both in the USWA and the WWF.

title. But two weeks later, Lawler won the title back from Mark.

After losing to Lawler, Mark went back to Texas to compete in USWA events there. He changed his wrestling name to the Punisher.

On October 5, 1989, Mark defeated Eric Embry for the USWA Texas Heavyweight Championship. On October 20, Mark lost the title to Kerry Adkisson. Adkisson wrestled as Kerry Von Erich.

Mark held each of these two championships only about two weeks. But his losses did not discourage him. Mark had been in the USWA only about six months and had already won two championships.

Mark often wrestled Jerry Lawler in the USWA.

Chapter 3

Early Success

Other professional wrestling companies noticed Mark's success. In early 1990, the National Wrestling Alliance (NWA) offered Mark a contract. This company later became WCW. Mark moved to Atlanta, Georgia, to wrestle for the NWA.

New Opportunities

Mark joined the NWA as a heel named Mean Mark Callous. Mark often broke rules to win matches. He sometimes hit his opponents with metal chairs or other props.

Mark soon joined a popular NWA tag team. Dan Spivey and Sid Eudy were known as the

Mark had several wrestling names before becoming the Undertaker.

> They [NWA officials] told me I'd never
> draw a dime in this business. They said
> I would never make it, and that
> I'd be a mid-carder at best.
> —Mark Callaway, *Dallas Morning News,* 10/8/99

Skyscrapers. Eudy wrestles as Psycho Sid Vicious. Vicious was hurt in a match and could not wrestle. Mark replaced Vicious as Spivey's partner. The team became known as the New Skyscrapers.

Mark and Spivey did well together. They won several matches, but Spivey then quit the NWA. Mark went back to competing alone.

In July 1990, Mark got a chance to wrestle for the NWA United States Championship. He wrestled champion Larry Pfohl at the Great American Bash in Baltimore, Maryland. Pfohl wrestles as Lex Luger. Mark was much larger than Luger, but Mark still lost the match. Later that summer, Mark wrestled Luger again for the U.S. title. Mark lost this match as well.

In fall 1990, the NWA chose not to renew Mark's contract. But Mark's wrestling career was not over. Mark met with Vince McMahon. McMahon owns the WWF. In November 1990, McMahon signed Mark to a contract.

Mark replaced Sid Vicious in the New Skyscrapers. Later, Mark and Vicious both wrestled in the WWF.

A New Start

WWF officials decided that Mark needed a new character and a new look. They came up with a character called the Undertaker. Many years ago, funeral directors were called undertakers. In the ring, Mark dressed like an Old West undertaker from the late 1800s. He wore a long black overcoat and a black hat. Organ music played as he walked into the ring.

Mark competed in the Royal Rumble in January 1991.

On November 22, 1990, Mark wrestled his first WWF match at Survivor Series in Hartford, Connecticut. Mark took part in a four-on-four elimination match with seven other wrestlers. Mark wrestled with Ted DiBiase, Greg Valentine, and Roy Farris. Farris wrestled as the Honky Tonk Man. Their opponents were Virgil Runnels Jr., Bret Hart, Jim Neidhart, and David Ware. Runnels wrestled as Dusty Rhodes. Ware wrestled as Koko B. Ware.

Mark did well in his first WWF match. He pinned Ware in less than two minutes. He then pinned Rhodes. Only two wrestlers were left on the other team. But Mark kept hitting Rhodes instead of trying to pin Hart and Neidhart. The referee disqualified Mark. DiBiase won the match.

In January 1991, Mark competed in the Royal Rumble. Mark tossed Bret Hart, Kerry Von Erich, and Butch Miller out of the ring. Joseph Laurinaitis and Michael Hegstrand then teamed up to throw Mark out of the ring. Laurinaitis and Hegstrand wrestled as the Legion of Doom.

An Old Friend

Bruce Prichard managed Mark when Mark joined the WWF. Prichard was known as Brother Love. In early 1991, Mark decided he needed a new manager. He remembered his friend William Moody from his early days of wrestling in Texas. Mark asked Moody to manage him.

> Don't let people tell you that you can't achieve something because you're different. It's OK to be different as long as you do it without hurting anyone.
> —Mark Callaway, *Milwaukee Journal Sentinel,* 10/18/98

Moody soon became one of the most famous managers in the WWF. He took the name "Paul Bearer." A pallbearer is a person who helps carry a coffin at a funeral.

During matches, Bearer wore white makeup on his face and dark makeup around his eyes. He brought smoky pots and containers called urns to the ring. Bearer said the pots and urns contained Mark's secret powers.

Mark and Bearer worked well together. Soon, some fans began to cheer for Mark.

More Success

On March 24, 1991, Mark celebrated both his birthday and one of his biggest matches yet. At WrestleMania 7, he wrestled James Reiher. Reiher is known as Jimmy "Superfly" Snuka. Mark used the Tombstone Piledriver to score his first WrestleMania victory.

Mark continued to win matches during the summer and fall of 1991. He defeated top WWF wrestlers such as James Hellwig. Hellwig wrestled as the Ultimate Warrior.

Paul Bearer became Mark's manager in 1991.

In November 1991, Mark competed for his first WWF title. He defeated Hulk Hogan at Survivor Series to become the WWF World Champion. Mark's championship lasted only one week. On December 3, Hogan defeated Mark to win back the title. But Mark had shown WWF officials and fans that he had the skills to be a top WWF wrestler.

Chapter 4

WWF Star

In early 1992, Mark's character changed from a heel to a babyface. Mark got involved in a match between Aurlian Smith Jr. and Randy Poffo. Smith wrestles as Jake "The Snake" Roberts. Poffo wrestles as "Macho Man" Randy Savage. During the match, Mark rescued Savage's wife, Miss Elizabeth. Mark's actions made him even more popular with the fans.

Trying for a Title

In 1992, Mark wrestled Ric Flair several times for the WWF World Championship. But he could not defeat Flair for the title.

Mark's Undertaker character has been both a heel and a babyface.

In January 1994, Mark had another chance at the World Championship. He wrestled Rodney Anoia at the Royal Rumble in Providence, Rhode Island. Anoia wrestled as Yokozuna. Mark and Yokozuna wrestled in a casket match. In this match, the first wrestler to lock his opponent into a casket wins.

Yokozuna was much larger than Mark. At the time, he weighed almost 600 pounds (272 kilograms). Yokozuna still needed the help of several other wrestlers to stuff Mark into the casket. Yokozuna won the match and kept the title.

In November 1994, Mark again faced Yokozuna in a casket match. This time, Mark defeated Yokozuna. But the match was not for the WWF World Championship.

In January 1996, Mark again wrestled for the WWF World Championship at the Royal Rumble. This time, his opponent was Bret Hart. During the match, Kevin Nash jumped in to help Hart. At the time, Nash wrestled as Diesel. The referee disqualified Hart because of Diesel's actions. But Hart still kept the title.

Yokozuna wrestled Mark in casket matches.

A Champion Again

On March 23, 1997, Mark again wrestled for the World Championship. He wrestled Sid Vicious at WrestleMania 13 in Chicago, Illinois. Late in the match, Bret Hart ran into the ring to help Mark. Mark then used a Tombstone Piledriver to pin Vicious. Mark was the WWF World Champion for the second time. This time, he was the fans' hero instead of a heel.

Rival in the Ring: Kane

Kane has been one of Mark's biggest rivals during the last several years. They have wrestled either as opponents or partners during many matches.

Kane's real name is Glen Jacobs. He is 7 feet (213 centimeters) tall and weighs 326 pounds (148 kilograms). Kane started wrestling in 1994. He joined the WWF in 1995 as Dr. Isaac Yankem. His first WWF appearance as Kane was October 5, 1997. His signature move is the chokeslam. Wrestling fans often call him the Big Red Machine.

In June 1998, Kane won the WWF World Championship by defeating Steve Austin at King of the Ring. Since then, he also has won the Hardcore Championship and the Intercontinental Championship. Like Mark, he is a successful tag team wrestler. He has won six WWF Tag Team titles. Two of those titles were with Mark. In fall 2001, Kane and Mark held both the WWF and WCW Tag Team titles.

Mark kept the title for more than three months. On August 3, Bret Hart challenged Mark for the title. Wrestler Michael Hickenbottom was the guest referee during this match. He wrestles as Shawn Michaels. Late in the match, Hart argued with Michaels. Michaels tried to hit Hart with a steel chair. Hart ducked. Michaels hit Mark instead. Hart then covered Mark for the pin and the title.

Reaching the Top

Mark's loss to Hart set up a cage match between Mark and Shawn Michaels on October 5, 1997. The match took place at Badd Blood in St. Louis, Missouri.

The ring was enclosed in a steel cage that was 16 feet (4.9 meters) tall. Both wrestlers were locked inside the cage.

During the match, Michaels knocked down a cameraman who was inside the cage. Referees opened the cage door to remove the cameraman. Michaels then escaped from the cage and climbed to the top. Mark followed him. He backdropped Michaels on the top of the cage. Mark later threw Michaels off the cage and into a table beside the ring. Mark then dragged

Michaels back into the cage. Michaels lay on the mat as Mark got ready to do a Tombstone Piledriver. Glen Jacobs then came to the cage. Jacobs wrestles as Kane. Kane ripped the door off the cage and took Mark down with a Tombstone Piledriver. Kane's actions cost Mark the match.

Mark wrestled Kane several times during 1998. On March 30, Mark defeated Kane at WrestleMania 14 in Boston, Massachusetts. On April 26, the two wrestlers met again at Unforgiven in Greensboro, North Carolina.

During this match, the edge of the ring was surrounded by fire. The two wrestlers jumped in and out of the ring as they struggled to breathe the hot air. At one point, Mark leaped over the flaming ropes and landed on top of Kane outside the ring. Mark defeated Kane.

A Great Match

On June 28, 1998, Mark wrestled a cage match that many wrestling fans consider one of the best of his career. His opponent was Mick Foley. Foley wrestled as Mankind.

Both men began the match by climbing to the top of the cage. Mark picked up Mankind

Many of Mark's best matches have been against Kane.

and threw him off the cage. Mankind crashed into the announcer's table. He lay there for several minutes before medical workers put him on a stretcher.

Mankind then got off the stretcher and climbed back to the top of the cage. Mark chokeslammed Mankind on top of the cage. Mankind fell through the cage into the ring as Mark jumped down after him. Mankind then left the ring and grabbed a bag of thumbtacks. He

In 1999, Mark dyed his hair black to make his character more mysterious.

spread them in the ring and prepared to slam Mark down on the tacks. But Mark chokeslammed Mankind on the tacks. Mark followed the chokeslam with a Tombstone Piledriver for the win.

Change in Character

Mark's character changed again in 1999. He still was called the Undertaker, but his character became even more mysterious. He again was a heel. Mark dressed in black, hooded robes. He dyed his hair black. He also formed a group of heels called the Ministry of Darkness.

On May 23, 1999, Mark had another chance to wrestle for the WWF World Championship. Mark's opponent was Steve Williams. Williams wrestles as "Stone Cold" Steve Austin. Paul Bearer and the referee helped Mark during the match. The referee was Vince McMahon's son, Shane.

Late in the match, Austin hit Mark with a chair. Mark fell to the mat. Austin covered Mark for the pin. Mark kicked out. Vince McMahon then came into the ring to help Austin. Austin took Mark down with a Stone Cold Stunner. Austin stood in front of Mark and wrapped his arms around Mark's head. He then dropped to his knees as he slammed Mark to the mat. Vince tried to count the fall, but Shane stopped him. Mark then covered Austin for a fast three-count. Mark was the WWF World Champion for the third time.

Chapter 5

The Undertaker Today

By fall 1999, Mark's years of wrestling had hurt his neck and back. He took some time off from wrestling to allow the injuries to heal.

In May 2000, Mark was well enough to wrestle again. The WWF again changed Mark's character. He still was called the Undertaker. But he no longer used coffins and urns as props. Instead, he rode a motorcycle into the ring. He wore jeans, a leather coat, and a bandanna.

Mark also had a new signature move, the Last Ride. For this move, Mark puts his

Mark's character changed again in 2000.

opponent's head between his knees. Mark flips the opponent's body to a sitting position on top of Mark's shoulders. Mark then lifts his opponent and slams the opponent straight down on the mat.

Most pro wrestling fans liked the change in Mark's character. He again became a babyface.

More Championships

Mark has wrestled many tag team matches since he returned to the ring in May 2000. On December 18, 2000, he teamed with Dwayne Johnson to win the WWF Tag Team Championship. Johnson wrestles as The Rock.

On August 19, 2001, Mark and Kane won the WWF Tag Team Championship. Mark and Kane had won the WCW Tag Team title two weeks earlier. They held both titles until September 2001.

Mark won another championship in 2001. On December 9, he defeated Rob Swatkowski for the WWF Hardcore Championship. Swatkowski wrestles as Rob Van Dam. Mark held the Hardcore title until February 5, 2002. He lost the title to Maven Huffman.

Mark remains one of the WWF's top wrestlers.

On March 17, 2002, Mark defeated Ric
Flair in a nontitle match at WrestleMania 18.
The win was Mark's 10th straight victory
at WrestleMania. Mark has never lost at
this event.

Outside the Ring
Mark still lives in Texas. He spends time with
his family when he is not wrestling. Mark has

Mark likes to ride motorcycles on the WWF TV shows and at his home in Texas.

two sons with his first wife, Jody. Gunner was born in 1993. Kevin was born in 1996.

Mark and Jody divorced in 1999. Mark married again in July 2000. His second wife's name is Sara. Sara sometimes appears with Mark on the WWF's TV shows.

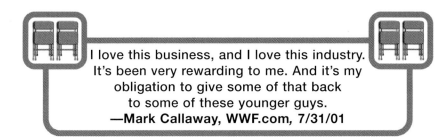

I love this business, and I love this industry. It's been very rewarding to me. And it's my obligation to give some of that back to some of these younger guys.
—Mark Callaway, WWF.com, 7/31/01

Like his character, Mark likes to ride motorcycles. Mark bought his first new motorcycle after he won his first WWF World Championship. He and Sara often ride their motorcycles near their home in Texas.

Mark has done some acting. He acted with Hulk Hogan in the 1991 movie *Suburban Commando*. He also appeared in the TV show *Poltergeist: The Legacy*.

Mark has had a long career in pro wrestling. He knows a great deal about the wrestling business. Other wrestlers say they consider him a leader. Mark often helps younger wrestlers with their moves and gives them advice. He may continue to work in the wrestling business after his wrestling career is over.

Career Highlights

1965 — Mark is born March 24 in Texas.

1983–1986 — Mark plays basketball for Angelina College and Texas Wesleyan University.

1989 — Mark wins two USWA championships.

1991 — Mark joins the WWF and defeats Hulk Hogan to win his first WWF World Championship.

1997 — Mark defeats Sid Vicious to win his second WWF World Championship.

1998 — Mark teams with Steve Austin to win the WWF Tag Team Championship.

1999 — Mark becomes the WWF Champion for the third time after defeating Steve Austin; he also wins two WWF Tag Team titles with the Big Show.

2000 — Mark teams with The Rock to win the WWF Tag Team Championship.

2001 — Mark teams with Kane to win both the WWF and WCW tag team titles; Mark also defeats Rob Van Dam for the WWF Hardcore Championship.

Words to Know

casket (KASS-kit)—a long, narrow box into which a dead person is placed for burial

contract (KON-trakt)—a legal agreement between a wrestler and a wrestling company

disqualify (diss-KWOL-uh-fye)—to prevent someone from taking part in or winning an activity; athletes can be disqualified for breaking the rules of their sport.

referee (ref-uh-REE)—a person who makes sure athletes follow the rules of a sport

scholarship (SKOL-ur-ship)—a grant of money that helps a student pay for education costs

signature move (SIG-nuh-chur MOOV)—the move for which a wrestler is best known; this move also is called a finishing move.

urn (URN)—a vase with a base; most urns are used as containers.

To Learn More

Alexander, Kyle. *Pro Wrestling's Most Punishing Finishing Moves.* Pro Wrestling Legends. Philadelphia: Chelsea House, 2001.

Hunter, Matt. *Superstars of Men's Pro Wrestling.* Male Sports Stars. Philadelphia: Chelsea House, 1998.

Molzahn, Arlene Bourgeois. *Mankind: Pro Wrestler Mick Foley.* Pro Wrestlers. Mankato, Minn.: Capstone High-Interest Books, 2002.

Ross, Dan. *The Story of the Wrestler They Call "the Undertaker."* Pro Wrestling Legends. Philadelphia: Chelsea House, 2000.

Useful Addresses

Professional Wrestling Hall of Fame
P.O. Box 434
Latham, NY 12110

World of Wrestling Magazine
P.O. Box 500
Missouri City, TX 77459-9904

World Wrestling Entertainment, Inc.
1241 East Main Street
Stamford, CT 06902

Internet Sites

Professional Wrestling Hall of Fame
http://www.pwhf.org

Professional Wrestling Online Museum
http://www.wrestlingmuseum.com/home.html

Undertaker.com
http://www.undertaker.com

WWE.com
http://www.wwe.com

Index

Austin, Steve, 30, 35

Badd Blood, 31–32
Bearer, Paul, 6–7, 24, 35

cage match, 31–34
Callaway, Sara, 40–41
casket match, 28
college, 11–12

Hogan, Hulk, 5–8, 25, 41

Kane, 8, 30, 32, 38

Last Ride, 37–38
Lawler, Jerry, 14, 17

Mankind, 32–34
Master of Pain, 14
McMahon, Vince, 20, 35
Mean Mark Callous,
   19–20
Michaels, Shawn, 31–32

National Wrestling
   Alliance (NWA), 15,
   19–20
New Skyscrapers, 19–20

Punisher, the, 17

Survivor Series, 5–8,
   22–23, 25

Tombstone Piledriver, 6,
   8, 24, 29, 32, 34

United States Wrestling
   Alliance (USWA), 14,
   15, 17

Von Erich, Fritz, 15

World Championship
   Wrestling (WCW), 8,
   19, 38
WrestleMania, 24, 29, 32,
   39